Little People, **BIG DREAMS**™

VANESSA NAKATE

Written by
Maria Isabel Sánchez Vegara

Illustrated by
Olivia Amoah

Frances Lincoln
Children's Books

In the African city of Kampala, the capital of Uganda, lived a little girl called Vanessa. She was the eldest of five siblings. Her parents always encouraged her to do what she thought was right and to raise her voice for a good cause.

When she grew up, Vanessa went to school in the countryside. The only time that her teacher talked to the class about climate change, it seemed like it was a problem on the other side of the world.

But, at college, Vanessa started noticing how floods and droughts destroyed crops, leaving families with nothing to eat. Africans were the least responsible for climate change, yet they were suffering the most!

Luckily, all over the world, millions of children were striking against climate change.

So, Vanessa convinced her siblings and cousins to join them, too. And even though no one paid much attention to them on the first day they protested, she didn't give up.

Two weeks later, she became the first child in her family to graduate from college, making her parents very proud.

GREEN LOVE

Still, all her aunties could think about was finding a fiancé for her and planning a wedding...

Whether she was alone or accompanied by friends, Vanessa continued with her weekly strikes. She raised her voice against the destruction of the Congolian rain forests, home to many people and animals.

SAVE CONGO
RAINF

SAVE CONGO
RAINFOREST

One day, she received an invitation to visit New York City
and join other young climate activists on a mission:
to convince world leaders to act against global warming.
No one in her family had ever traveled that far before.

Vanessa made friends, attended meetings, and even joined a massive climate march. Yet, somehow, she still felt alone.

There is NO PLANET B

SAVE CONGO RAINFOREST

PEO
Ov
PRO

HOUSE
N FIRE

PROTECT OUR FUTURE

CLIMA

CLIMATE
STRIKE

JUST

She was one of the few African activists there, and not much was said about how global warming was affecting her continent.

SAVE CONGO RAINFOREST

Back home, there was a lot of work to do! Vanessa organized cleanups, talked to students about global warming, wrote an open letter to Uganda's president, and started a project to bring eco-friendly stoves and solar energy to schools.

Vanessa joined a handful of activists at a protest in Switzerland. She thought it would give her a chance to share her story, but, after checking the news, Vanessa realized that her words had been left out and her image had been removed from a photograph.

She felt like her whole continent had been erased from the conversation about global warming. But instead of giving up and going back home quietly, Vanessa decided to speak up about being ignored. And this time, the world listened.

From that day on, her words sounded louder than ever. She signed articles, took part in lectures, and wrote a book about being a climate activist.

Soon, she was recognized as one of the most influential young Africans of the year.

And today, little Vanessa is not just a strong voice against climate change in her continent. She is also an inspiration to girls who dream of leading Africa, and the whole of our planet, to a brighter future.

CLIMATE JUSTICE

THERE IS NO PLANET B

PROTECT OUR WATER

SAVE THE AMAZO

GREEN LOVE

VANESSA NAKATE

(Born 1996)

2020   2021

Born in the Ugandan city of Kampala, Vanessa Nakate was the eldest of five children. Growing up, she noticed that education about climate change was almost completely absent from the school education system in her country. When she learned about Greta Thunberg's School Strike for Climate, she was inspired to herself strike outside the Ugandan parliament. After several months, other teenagers began to respond to her social-media posts and the Young for Future Africa movement was formed. Her protests drew international attention to the vast deforestation happening to the Congo Basin, which contains the second largest rain forest in the world. Soon, Vanessa was invited to speak at international conferences and called for an immediate end to the use of energy that is harmful to the environment. She also started the Green Schools Project,

2022   2022

a renewable-energy initiative that helps Ugandan schools transition to using solar energy and eco-stoves. In January 2020, Vanessa was cropped out of a photo that she appeared in with other young climate activists and her outrage sparked media attention. She said, "You didn't just erase a photo. You erased a continent… Africans have truly been erased from the map of climate change." Vanessa raised her voice about the injustice of being erased, and the world listened. She continues to meet world leaders and climate activists to bring attention to the impact of climate change on Africa. An inspirational leader and a voice of hope, Vanessa teaches the world that using your voice is the most powerful tool for change, and we must all use our voices to build a brighter future for the world.

Want to find out more about **Vanessa Nakate?**

Have a read of this great book:

We Have a Dream: Meet 30 Young Indigenous People and People of Colour Protecting the Planet by Dr Mya-Rose Craig and Sabrena Khadija

Brimming with creative inspiration, how-to projects, and useful information to enrich your everyday life, quarto.com is a favourite destination for those pursuing their interests and passions.

Published by Peter Marley • Designed by Lyli Feng
Comissioned by Lucy Menzies • Edited by Rachel Robinson
Production by Nikki Ingram

Manufactured in Guangdong, China CC112022
1 3 5 7 9 8 6 4 2

Photographic acknowledgements (pages 28-29, from left to right): 1. Climate activists Vanessa Nakate, from left, Luisa Neubauer, Greta Thunberg, Isabelle Axelsson, and Loukina Tille arrive for a news conference on the closing day of the World Economic Forum (WEF) in Davos, Switzerland, on Friday, Jan. 24, 2020. World leaders, influential executives, bankers and policy makers attend the 50th annual meeting of the World Economic Forum in Davos from Jan. 21 – 24 © Simon Dawson/Bloomberg via Getty Images. 2. Ugandan climate activist Vanessa Nakate is pictured within an interview with AFP on the sidelines of the Youth4Climate event on September 29, 2021 in Milan. © Miguel Medina/AFP via Getty Images. 3. STOCKHOLM, SWEDEN - JUNE 3: Climate activist Vanessa Nakate attends a protest organized by Fridays for Future against perceived inaction by governments towards climate change on June 03, 2022 in Stockholm, Sweden. Climate activist organizations, including Fridays For Future, protested on the side-lines of the Stockholm50+ climate summit in Stockholm, and the youth-led Aurora movement announced details of their legal action against the Swedish state in relation to their climate policies. © Jonas Gratzer/Stringer via Getty Images. 4. Vanessa Nakate poses for a photo at the Unicef office in New York on September 14, 2022. - Newly appointed UNICEF Goodwill Ambassador, the young climate activist Vanessa Nakate has made it her mission to "amplify" the voices of children on the frontlines of global warming, so that their suffering is not just "statistics". © Ed Jones/AFP via Getty Images.

Collect the *Little People*, **BIG DREAMS**™ series:

FRIDA KAHLO · COCO CHANEL · MAYA ANGELOU · AMELIA EARHART · AGATHA CHRISTIE · MARIE CURIE · ROSA PARKS · AUDREY HEPBURN

EMMELINE PANKHURST · ELLA FITZGERALD · ADA LOVELACE · JANE AUSTEN · GEORGIA O'KEEFFE · HARRIET TUBMAN · ANNE FRANK · MOTHER TERESA

JOSEPHINE BAKER · L. M. MONTGOMERY · JANE GOODALL · SIMONE DE BEAUVOIR · MUHAMMAD ALI · STEPHEN HAWKING · MARIA MONTESSORI · VIVIENNE WESTWOOD

MAHATMA GANDHI · DAVID BOWIE · WILMA RUDOLPH · DOLLY PARTON · BRUCE LEE · RUDOLF NUREYEV · ZAHA HADID · MARY SHELLEY

MARTIN LUTHER KING JR. · DAVID ATTENBOROUGH · ASTRID LINDGREN · EVONNE GOOLAGONG · BOB DYLAN · ALAN TURING · BILLIE JEAN KING · GRETA THUNBERG

JESSE OWENS · JEAN-MICHEL BASQUIAT · ARETHA FRANKLIN · CORAZON AQUINO · PELÉ · ERNEST SHACKLETON · STEVE JOBS · AYRTON SENNA

LOUISE BOURGEOIS · ELTON JOHN · JOHN LENNON · PRINCE · CHARLES DARWIN · CAPTAIN TOM MOORE · HANS CHRISTIAN ANDERSEN · STEVIE WONDER

MEGAN RAPINOE · MARY ANNING · MALALA YOUSAFZAI · ANDY WARHOL · RUPAUL · MICHELLE OBAMA · MINDY KALING · IRIS APFEL

ROSALIND FRANKLIN · RUTH BADER GINSBURG · MARILYN MONROE · KAMALA HARRIS · ALBERT EINSTEIN · CHARLES DICKENS · YOKO ONO · MICHAEL JORDAN

NELSON MANDELA · PABLO PICASSO · AMANDA GORMAN · GLORIA STEINEM · FLORENCE NIGHTINGALE · HARRY HOUDINI · J.R.R. TOLKIEN · ELVIS PRESLEY

NEIL ARMSTRONG · ALEXANDER VON HUMBOLDT · NIKOLA TESLA · WILMA MANKILLER · MARCUS RASHFORD · LAVERNE COX · MAE JEMISON · DWAYNE JOHNSON

HELEN KELLER · ANNA PAVLOVA · QUEEN ELIZABETH · TERRY FOX · HEDY LAMARR · SHAKIRA · FREDDIE MERCURY · LEWIS HAMILTON

LOUIS PASTEUR · PRINCESS DIANA · DAVID HOCKNEY · VANESSA NAKATE

Scan the QR code for free activity sheets, teachers' notes and more information about the series at www.littlepeoplebigdreams.com